THE
BELOVED

Andrew Hart Benson

NFB
Buffalo, New York

ISBN: 978-1-7338764-0-7

Beloved/Benson-1st ed.

1. Poems. 2. Poetry. 3. Verse.
4. Benson

NFB Publishing/Amelia Press
<<<>>>
119 Dorchester Road
Buffalo, New York 14213
        For more information please visit
        nfbpublishing.com

Preface

Whenever I'm feeling sad a wall is built in my mind. I try my best to scale it or find some way around it. But the wall stretches from corner to corner of my mind. I can distract myself with music or some blue eyed men on the internet. But no distraction can work. The wall stands until it doesn't. That is how it works. That is how it will always work.

The nature of this wall isn't self-defensive. It isn't protecting anyone. If anything it is self-hindering. I stop whatever I'm doing. I can sit for hours beside the wall. I can't focus. I can reach out to anything. The wall is strong, not superhero strong. It has the type of strength that can starve you if it wanted.

I'm talking as if I know this wall, as if I like it. I do. But for a while I didn't like the wall because I didn't like myself. Honestly, I hated it. I hated feeling helpless, worthless, and alone because of it. Nothing I did could breach the parapet. For years I pointed my finger at other people. I am this way because people push me away; they don't treat me the way I should be treated. I craved attention and felt embarrassed when I had it because either way the wall was up and I felt alone. The wall started getting higher and longer because it was all that I cared about. It was all-consuming; self-hindering.

There was a point in time when the wall had disappeared. I was given a new start. I was prideful, eager, and excited. It wasn't long until the wall was built again. I don't know why. It is just how it works. I felt comfortable behind the wall because I had been there for so long. It was quiet too; simple. A part of me knew that no matter the situation, the wall would always rebuild itself along with the craving for attention, the embarrassment, and the feelings of worthlessness, helplessness, and loneliness.

With the comfortability of being trapped behind a wall there was a knowledge too. I could predict once the cycle would repeat itself; what I would feel and when I would feel it. But I was always caught off guard when it came. As the cycle repeated and I saw the wall being built and unbuilt, I learned what guided me through it: love.

I had a growing affection for the people around me, art, and shirtless men. Every time the wall would build and rebuild itself it is those things that watched me. I found the passion and fire that was in all things. This love and affection, even with the conflicting emotions and drama, could crack the wall at any moment and keep it standing. So often I found myself writing and dreaming about sadness because it is the passion I found to be what I loved. It was then that I could paint the wall with shades of reds, blues, and purples. It was this growing relationship and friendship with depression that has helped me manage it.

I say manage because depression is not something I have to cure, it is something I have to manage. It isn't something I need to expel because it is a part of myself. I had to grow to love myself and find the love in things in order to combat my depression. Although the feeling of sadness may be self-hindering, I have learned how to make it beloved.

Introduction

The Beloved captures the essence of overcoming a mental illness. For me, the key to balancing the difficulties of a mental illness and the trials of life is love. Love and passion is what gets me through the day, whether sad or not. Accepting what you have is the hardest thing to do, but it is the only way to manage depression. Finding the passion within the people that I connect with, the art that I admire and the emotions tied to them keep me from being buried behind the wall forever.

Each character represents some of the loves of my life. Dominic represents coming to terms with finding my voice. As an ordinary suburban boy, I was forced into local sports. I hated it and I had to find out where I felt the most prideful. I had to find my voice. Lucas details the struggles with self-acceptance and self-love. It took me a long time to overcome serious doubt in myself. It wasn't until I broke out of high school and into new environments that I found myself thriving. Connor describes the home writing always has in my heart. Ever since I was little, I naturally wrote my ideas down. I would never stop creating, never stop writing ideas down, and never stop dreaming. Mac deals with society. There is a struggle to conform to society, to feel at a distance from it, and to accept it. I was a part of theatre in high school, this serves as inspiration for most of Mac. Being on stage is both intimate and lonely. The audience is seeing you when you're most vulnerable in a collective space but you're alone up there on stage and you have no way of escaping either aspect.

Susan B talks about Rochester, my hometown. It is the place that I changed the most in. However, it is also the place I feel desperate to leave. Susan B is all about history; my history. Alex is about the men in my life. In her chapter I detail the struggle to come to terms with the men in my life. I struggle to love them, to want them, to accept them, and to leave them. Alex finds her place in my heart and helps me be comfortable enough to feel all of this. Jo details the media and its powers. The media can change how we think about people, ourselves, and the world. It is fascinating. Scary mostly. Jensen is a mystery to me and I love it. Lastly, Sasha describes the environment. There is something wonderful about a place that is crafted like a film set. As if everything was placed to fit a certain mood and emotion. This love of places and their feelings is all what Sasha is about.

Hopefully, all of these passions find their way in the corners of different minds. Instead of focusing on the suppressing weight that mental illness bares. Use that weight to drive your passions and feel something truly beloved.

DOMINIC

<u>Find the courage</u>

Do I seem dumb if I don't say it? He never thought it because he never guessed it. I think this every time I wake up. Like an instinct. When I dream it seems that my mouth is sewed shut. The only way to open it is to wake up. I can't speak. I can't write a message in the snow or the weeds. No one believes me. Then I wake up. Like an instinct. And I am paralyzed like an instinct. My neck pulls forward to search for the words. I found one! It comes out in an ooh or eee. But my neck pulls forward for the rest of the day. Struggling to find the words that dream in the space. It surprises me. The moment my mouth breaks I am full of courage. I need social contact but my mind flops the race. It cannot keep up. It will not stay be. I am lucky if my emotions start to surface. I am not lying when I say my words are worthless. I need to share a presence. I need to soak in the scene. I may not say much but my words are there, lurking. It takes me a while to find the words in the waste. But now I have to choose what to say. What do I say? Who will I be? Reveal just enough for you to be seen.

<u>To share</u>

I share parts of myself when I'm comfortable. It's like a pop quiz. What do I share? Which parts are most loveable? Which parts do I keep hidden? What I say could be wrong. These are the words I'll have to wear. So I could refrain from risk and keep them at a distance. But if I don't say a thing I'll be unwritten. Just like that I could disappear. If I say the right thing I could be memorable. Say something and it will be suitable. I could squeeze out every last drop of my muse. Squeeze out everything that is latent. Squeeze out these things and I'll be labeled as sin. Not really, but just as so. After this chance I may never talk again. But if I am given this chance should I be discursive and open? Refrain from risk and avoid failure. Censor my muses. Cover the bruises.

When politicians are on TV they have a script to say. It holds a certain message, one they can rephrase. They silence the world by taking the stage. They silence the opposition. They censor their muses and cover their bruises. They reveal just enough for their voice to persuade. Why is it that saying your knowledge is what proves you have it? When so many of us often take the stage. Why try to impress or worry about comments. When all you should worry about is if you are safe on that stage.

Do I seem dumb if I don't say it? I may seem dumb either way.

LUCAS

<u>I put on a façade</u>

I put on a façade
When someone says I have another,
Their words describe what they see
And I take it as a blunder.
Most remarks degrade my character
Even if their intent
Was to speak some truth on what I'm ignoring.

I put on a façade
When I say I loved our time
It was better apart than it was entwined
I've got no alibi.
I find I'm often alone in the streets
So how could you know my kind?
I've got no alibi.

<u>The first time someone saw the cuts on my arm</u>

The first time someone saw the cuts on my arm
I felt the world take a look at me,
I heard all the conversations they would say,
If they asked why I wouldn't know,
I made countless reasons to deflect their questions:
"It just happened once,
I was drunk,
It didn't feel good,"
And then no one asked.

There was never a conversation had,
I felt lonelier than ever,
I didn't know why I cut myself,
The physical pain did not match my emotional pain,
It seemed as though there was no cure;
No one to help,
No one who cared,
All they had to do was ask.
Maybe then I could've figured things out sooner.

All I really wanted was for someone's effort,
A simple 'are you okay?' is never enough.
I would've thought adults were good at this,
But it turns out my peers understood better.
It was hidden from my friends,
It was hidden from the world after I showed them.
This conversation wasn't had because people were scared,
This conversation should be had because I was scared;
Show effort to your family or friends who are scared.

<u>There was a certain special day in May</u>

There was a certain special day in May
When I knew the time, song, and place.
As the days blew by I relieved the pain
From the words that my mom would say,
And my dad said as well,
And the ignorance that presided them both.

I left the second place without a trace
And took time to find a more positive place.
I packed my bags and walked away
From the sadness that this place conveyed.
All my friends then wished me well
And others didn't notice that I digressed to speak.

I finally escaped the first place that caused me so much shame,
The more and more people pushing me under my way,
The idea that the good times will start forgave,
The excuse to rot in this excuse for a learning place.
With my cap and gown I reminded myself
That this graduation is a bargaining chip.

The anniversary of the day in May,

I got a note on my phone to remind me to rage,

I let it control the evening at my favorite café,

I forced myself into this disobey;

Sulking in the sheets of my thoughts,

Sulking right next to the spot where I lost my shot.

It was just hours from the end of the day in May;

As I lotion dried tears that spread on my face,

I sat in my bathroom crafting a play,

I listened to songs that convinced me to stay awake,

I forgot their ignorance as my parents spoke,

The day in May had been just another for both.

<u>I have changed</u>

I have changed
And I'm glad that the few of you have stuck around,
I was lost, silly, and in need of a path to follow;
The decisions of people would confuse me inside.
I've said some stupid things but you still smiled,
Then made fun of me and found fun in the honesty.

I have changed
And I'm glad I am able to tell some of you how;
All the streets that I crossed and the people I've met,
The lessons I've learned from the pain in my life,
How I continue to put a smile on my face,
And hope to do the same for you people in my space.

I have changed
And I'm glad that some of you haven't seen it.
Left me sorry, oblivious, and uncomfortable,
Too young to know the world and all of its true,
You moved on while I was mourning you,
Now you're left in my thoughts for my muse.

I have changed
But I'm happy to remember all of you.

CONNOR

I know this may seem odd,
I know I will sound bleak,
This is how I can convey my mind confidently.
I'm not asking for a break
Just to meet me in the middle,
Even glancing at these pages are worth you stepping
To belittle.

I write this song to you
With many more to come.
Played along with a big symphonic drum
I write my love, adieu,
Find it in your heart to understand me;
My dying wish while we both pass,
Onward, to find peace.

Here is a few detailed instructions for you,
Grab your paper,
Grab your pen,
And your computer too.
Here is a few detailed instructions for you,
Take notes,
I'm not trying to amuse.

<u>Detailed Instructions 2</u>

It doesn't seem a single moment we'll be separately
Scouring to find a crossroad sovereignty;
Our slogan for our love candidacy,
My slogan to survive this matrimony:
Come meet me.

It's good to start with no fallacy,
Only fall in love with who I'll be,
As a man who loves a man I know they will be weary,
Take my hand, I command, and get to know me:
I'm shakey.

I'm the furnace that you're burning inside;
You're my fuel –a compliment by design,
I like to argue for I can't pick a side,
Just walk me through it:
Justify.

Think twice before you apologize,
Think right away don't criticize,
I can snap at any time I'd like,
Just talk me through it:
Sanctify.

Think soon mental health isn't kind.
Think clue number two's in this next rhyme,
If Alice would've never judged the rabbit,
Would she have a friend to tell her the time?
It's masochratic!

Think now before I start to cry,
Don't try to control my leery eyes,
Thought life could end in a lonely night,
I wished to die for the latter half of life:
Sociopathic.

I have never been forced in line,
This way of living might be alright,
Thought life could end in a lonely night,
I've felt alive for this last half of life:
Enigmatic.

I'm not afraid to say what's on my mind,
Sometimes I don't make sense, I get wild,
Like criminals I deserve a fair trial,
You treat me as such like I dressed for that style,
You're signed on –don't be in it for the mile,
I'll be with you and never staying idle.

Did your pen run off like the words I try to phrase?

Every word I got can't be written on one page,

Would you believe me if matter couldn't change,

The chemicals inside that make my brain change its game,

It's useless to compute this into zeros, ones, and blame,

I take full responsibility for this spectacle on stage.

Don't hold it with your hand I'm not finished yet,

You've held tips in your lips much bigger than this,

Would you believe me if I didn't plan this trick?

It was our genes who dreamed they could convict,

An innocent boy with a hungry barbarian,

This letter puts me in the middle –come meet me totalitarian.

It seems like I'm finished with my first detailed instructions,

No teaser,

No promo,

This is my introduction.

I know we may be stuck together,

But hopefully not forever,

Read this out loud,

Tell me what you think,

Detailed instructions in the middle for mending.

Detailed Instructions 3

Getting closer is hard to do
So here are some moments of you,
They're my favorite in my head,
They're your favorite on the page,
This at least I know is true.

I snuck around when you least expected,
Held your hand to keep you invested,
I followed you all day in my head,
I followed my heart,
Your hands I would ring in vested.

We didn't have to make clear what stares meant,
My glasses were fogged by my willing consent,
We kept quiet in the bathroom stall,
We kept fucking up and down the wall,
And every time after we did without discontent.

Stuck around for when I finished a book,
Tears made a puddle in the binding's crook,
I could never let go of the characters,
I could never let go of the words,
But your shoulder let me keep them.

~31~

Together we arranged a nightly routine;
Your face stay smothered in the sheets unseen,
Waiting for me to finish my cleanse,
Waiting for my hand to grab in reflex,
Together are routine became libertine.

We whispered all night till our breath was laconic,
Our comments and tongues rolled out a mnemonic;
If I'm by your side when you fall asleep,
When we're apart I will be in your dreams,
This can cleanse love that's toxic.

I listened as your ideas came flooding through,
Sculpting and shading the perfect hue,
Both are perspectives ignite a movement,
In our families who think two boys can't choose men,
We lay on the floor laughing till our bodies turn blue.

Surprised me at work when you were low,
My company is better than being alone,
Coworkers marveled at the ardor in air,
Coworker's candor began to haunt,
We depend on each other much more than we know.

I trusted you to love me bare,
To beat, hold, and control me but stop with a stare,
As long as I was safe you were to do as you please,
No look askance could satisfy your need,
Like this we could watch the world burn without care.

You could find me thinking under the moon,
Colors and thoughts entwined in the loom,
Choose the right stitch to keep me together,
We know how people get in the full moon light,
This place we love engraved in cotton rune.

We exchanged the songs we would sing on stage,
Bartered small pieces of our soul as a wage,
All of these things and my life's undone,
All of these things make me see love,
Sue me for resisting to turn the page.

Detailed instructions for the likes of you,
Hopefully one day you'll read them too,
But for now you'll exist in my head,
And actual in the lines of these pages,
This at least I hope to be true.

<u>Detailed Instructions 4</u>

Don't let these pages be my legacy,
They can't speak for me,
I may be telling you this with great confidence
But I c-c-can't.
I even stutter on these pages.
I even blame myself for leaving.
When I turn red and start to sweat
You're the only thing I have left.
Sanctify the breach in confidence
Tackle it with being compassionate.
Take what I say,
Take what I write,
The purity of the moment,
And the essence of the memory.
Combine them both;
This is my legacy.
Not a poet,
Not a writer,
Not a nervous wreck,
Not a fighter.
This poem lacks structure
But it's the most honest I will be.
In these words,
Within these lines,
From my body
And from my dreams
I'm letting you in
Embrace the love and give it back to me.

~34~

Detailed Instructions 5

History books can't comprehend it,
We call it mental health awareness,
You've read up on every page I've written
And now I'll thank you with this last submission.

Some people run away from me
When they see me stuttering,
They say "look at him, he's sweating
He's a mess, I hope this kid is joking."
I'm glad you've seen a side from me
Not my red face beating,
My nonsense-ical mutterings,
My anxiety that you keep guarding.

I'm happy to admit the best thing for me
Is the man who lets me stare at him endlessly,
We love attention and we share it conveniently,
I speak with my mouth when my mind is done talking.
That's why I love the paper, pen, my efficacy.

I'm happy to admit this isn't then end,
You can burn all these pages till your lighters content,
But the ink I've spilled will act as a vex,
It's a conclusion from one end to the next,
I'm not afraid of all the things I have confessed.
Are you?

MAC

<u>Apart of the Scene</u>

I can't sing
But I kept dreaming –I kept faking,
I kept quiet and stayed blending in,
I can't sing but I can sure fake it.

I can't dance,
My feet can't think of things in advance,
I get nervous –get locked in a stance,
It's mostly from the mental cell block prance.

And I can't act,
I feel aghast when I'm asked to react,
Leave me sheltered underneath the black,
My presence makes up for what I lack.

Apart of the scene,
I'm a boy in need of something I can reach,
An eager heart but lost in anxiety,
Apart of the scene by means that agree.

Apart of a dream,
I can feel the doubt flow through my bloodstream,
This is no life to live we're made to scheme,
But this remains the only place where I believe.

Apart of the scene,
Just a weirdo on his journey.

<u>Headphones Loud</u>

I've always attracted gossip:
Skinny boy, theatre toy, and eccentric,
I could scream loud like a prophet,
I don't believe in what I pull from my pockets.

People deem me a crown of thorns,
That's funky, sometimes edgy, but not proud,
I can't help it that I dance to the sounds
Of the rhythms that make me stand out.

I've locked myself down with my headphones loud,
Panning from left to right in my mind.
Lyrics of love for the jitter bug,
How come this music soothes my mind?

I've never been attracted to progress,
A standstill heart lot but now I digress,
Just ignore what everyone else says,
Bury it deep under a hard surface.

The static can't cover the fragments,
Quick comments slip through a passage;
I'm denying the eventual lament,
Standing still till the heart lot turns to harlot.

Try to define it; to many people's comments,
Panning from left to right in my mind.
Lyrics of love make my dream more fun,
They say it'll heal with time,
But should I listen or resign?

<u>Typecast</u>

Do you know who you are?
They'll tell you,
In every sentence you spread,
They'll tell you,
Hold your arms a different way,
'You're not yourself,"
This is not your play,
And everyone has their wealth.

Read the words that are here,
Look at them,
Try to abide to them,
Look at them,
Bring your personal flare,
I'll adjust to my liking,
You can expand how you want,
But to the limits I am providing.

They'll tell you 'look at them,'
Like your capable of few things,
But with a wide range of talent,
Your stuck flying with clipped wings.

<u>The lights and the stage</u>

I look toward the lights
And see the people in their seats;
The program in their laps
And their money in sight.

Their faces are shadowed,
But I can feel they're keen;
Watching my every movement
And tying their lasso.

I look down the stage
And see the world that I thrive in,
It's part of the history book I make,
And it writes on my page.

Each set fills my head,
Like the memories from my past
And trespasses in every frame;
Where I lay in the dream bed.

The lights and the stage
Find ways to twist my mind;
In bright thoughts and dark tremors,
As ink quaint on the page.

―――――

SUSAN B

―――――

Friday the 13th

"Some things can be done as well as others"
It tries to be sold on newspaper covers.
Make a proclaim to cause outrage,
Across the Rochester land,
Sam Patch will jump the day death commands.

Do your toys start to bore you and start to hinder?
Do you want to see Sam jump into a river?
And entrusted will he be at the Genesee,
For his bear come to aid at his Calvary.

After highest fright at the falls of Niagara,
He plights at High Falls –abracadabra!
Is he gone? Is the dead? Is he lost in a cave?
Or in hells deepest falls as the devils slave?

His body feels the demons; it begins to shutter,
Or maybe from the solemn newspaper cover,
A jump to death on the worst day of the year,
Isn't his rationale a little bit queer?

Sam Patch soon became quite the spectacle on stage,
Every woman surveyed him as he would do the same,
The attention, the suspicion, and the constant remarks,
Made dear Sam realize this was only the start.

"Some things can be done as well as others"
This is the only quote Sam had on the cover,
Then soon he would scream it on stage,
To reach all ends of the promise land,
To watch the bravest man meet the end by his command.

Sam was whipped and in conviction he worked,
Until his very last day and what was it worth?
A high that lasted as long as his mighty jump
And enough to set ablaze inside of Sam's rump.

Some talents are had –some not others,
Yonder, a talent could muster,
Yonder and yonder Sam Patch explained,
Not a soul could see what he tried to refrain.

"Some things can be done as well as other"
It is sold on newspaper covers.
This proclaim has caused an outrage,
Across the Rochester land,
Sam Patch has died by death's command.

<u>Kodak</u>

Camera, camera,
Kodak camera,
Revamped today,
Still losing stamina,
American dogma,
Diminished dogma,
Eastman gardens,
Rose pricking with karma.

Gregarious, breathless,
Cigarette breathless,
Electronic cousins,
Are still killing countless,
Children are nest-less,
The streets keep them restless,
Where is their pride?
When all things aren't relished.

Camera, camera,
Kodak, camera,
Capture a moment,
Case for dysphoria,
The moxie aroma,
New techno aroma,
Breathes new lungs to life,
And kills old formula.

<u>July '64</u>

The echoes of howls filled the city,
The nightmares of teeth disturbed the night,
In the melting pot was a stew of fright,
In the seventh ward,
In July '64.

The harm of blacks both plagued and plenty,
The neighbors share the dimmed spotlight,
They're crowded in squares that mock their birthright,
In the seventh ward,
In the Rochester world.

The moonlit night started to rumble,
In drunken tumult they cry amidst,
The howls and teeth that haunt their eclipse,
They will settle score,
They're not hid from the world.

The riots tear the land they cherish,
Friends, family, and neighbors suffer,
They're locked in chains for helping smother,
In the seventh ward,
All the abuse ignored.

The truth is they wanted to be heard,
The injustices of smugtown co.,
And these actions that they should know,
Caused the biggest war,
In July '64.

<u>Lilac</u>

The lilacs of Highland Ave
Give word that summer's coming;
A natural and quaint dance
Of senses are inviting
Hummingbirds,
Butterflies,
Pools the color of the sky,
Matrimony,
Fair weather,
And next winter's disguise.

The lilacs of Highland Ave
Welcome the visitors marching.
Bring cheerful and wondrous glee,
Our friends from beyond these fields;
Cancer signs,
Leo roots,
Sailors in sea miles,
Stories unbound,
Sweet pleasure,
And the exchange's smile.

The lilacs of Highland Ave

Make homes for those wandering;

With more than four walls

And enough rooms to occupy;

Hoarded basements,

Empty beds,

Rooftops with sunset views,

Coffee kitchens,

Scented tubs,

With lots of love to pursue.

ALEX

Phantom Bruise

The king sat down to tell a tale of his
And how he used to whip who honored him.
We could never find a scar to credit his abuse,
We could never excuse from this phantom bruise.

The king sat down to drool a tale of his
And how he liked to rule his two civilians.
A reason for rebellion was always ignored,
No reason to leave, no bruise –no need for abscond.

All the time he stammered in faint armistice,
I'd be drafting in my head a correspondence,
His rhyme and reason was too eclectic,
My mind was racing trying to keep up with it.

The king sat down to tell this tale of time,
The damage he caused was inherently mine,
Love's got weights tied to my ankles in a pool,
Drowning while people are swimming cool.

The king sits down in this space of mine,
Speaking his thoughts like I'm his phantom shrine,
With golden wicks burning till their smoke,
My whispers will fade just like the smoke blows.

All the time that I blamed my uselessness,
I would be used if he was less of a pest,
Now my lover thinks that it's ridiculous,
That I'm the boy who's meant to be a princess.

All the time that I wasted hating him,
Was thrown away, I didn't mean it,
And now that you are good as dead,
I've got nothing left of you but a phantom bruise.

<u>Strangers in Public</u>

First time,
My big brown camera eyes,
Took snapshots to bring into bed with me,

Second time,
The spell you cast on my guise,
Who knows if he'll ever come back like this rhyme.

Seven at night,
Our smiles are dancing like light,
Strangers in public lust in denied conscious sight,

Four in the morning,
Lie awake with the sound of the ping,
Coming from a mechanic heart that's malfunctioning.

Fifth time I touch myself,
The absence of his body shows his wealth,
And no friends, good karma, or music can defeat the stealth,

Of the last time I saw him,
And the feelings buried deep within my whims,
That pull apart the lusting heart of one left companionless.

<u>Uncle Chuckles</u>

Pour another tasteless liquid,
As it slides through his teeth,
Wipe his mouth clean with your tongue,
Entangled like the vines of a heath,
Mother and father birth the world drunkenly,
Her head hanging on a wreath.
To decorate him when he needs
His family to see him thriving.

Give him a hurricane's eye,
He'll never be wrapped in a whirl,
As he sees through her desire,
Around her neck like her biggest pearl,
As he sees through their standards,
The noose his fingers start to curl,
Hanging down the world's neck;
Blowing winds and blowing swirls.

He wasn't made for this world,
But remedies they'll make him.
Whatever he wanted,
Vomits up pristine and prim,
Every soul is a mother's gift,
Altruism in every whim.
He wasn't made for this world,
But he knows how to fake it.

<u>Wingman of the bully</u>

So often I'm looked over,
I can't help but blush when eyes are on me,
For him I'm like every other body,
Just a prize for this ego-frantic godly,
Coward with the eyes of a mastermind,
Tender hands and disguised tender lies.

So often I do perceive,
As a babe that you can shoot down with pride,
I will quiver as you continue to stride.
For me it's a rollercoaster not a ride,
I'm tied down –can't call for cover,
And so used to it I might call you a lover,

So often lover you can't provide,
You've got your wingman and each other,
But we compete just like we're each other's brother,
These thoughts are swirling –good –bad, they like to smother,
I was lost in my ego centered dream,
Now I'm watching as it unfolds at the seams.

So I pluck those feathers right out of,
This arrogant wingman –you chose wrong,
Delirious visions of me cowering instead,
You'll be groaning because you're dead,
You're dead to me.

<u>Crocodile Kiss</u>

A smile is enough for this crock to pick,
A vagabond with pure happiness,
An instinct disguised as a mutual sin,
Oil his skin and love falls in,
To the ravine of one thing in common;
This momentary lust is just for us.

A Floridian with a traveling shtick,
And a loner who is left loveless,
I got what I could never honor,
Security of man with armor,
So lustful for my man –my sovereign,
But I knew it wasn't right.

The crock had this chance to be quick,
Had every upper hand with my innocence,
Every argument he could win,
He was breaking the doors of heaven,
All I could think of was letting him,
And I did without a fuss.

Crock fed others and acted slick,
The words he used –I like to digress,
Crock's age didn't prove he was smarter,
Keep ranting and put up your armor,
This crock won't dock at my harbor,
But still he could rock this boat.

Swampy eyes shed light to his gimmick,
Turn on the lights and forget to suppress,
My heart that longed to love for longer,
I'll listen to songs as the days get darker,
The end of summer can't come any sooner,
And the crock will be gone before I know it.

The winter days have left me lovesick,
Happy, calm, and tired of distress,
I knew we couldn't swim the same waters,
Crock's age wasn't an alibi to garner;
We just weren't from the same waters.

Boy on the Corner

He's another missed opportunity,
In my book.
Strung him by my curiosity,
With one look.
I played shook so I didn't have to say,
I was hooked but I restrained and stayed away.

I try to keep a faint serenity,
It's my cure.
I'll forget it like every calamity,
I'll stay pure.
At least in denial like my closeted life,
No club lust can wile my lonely nights.

It was my fault all along,
I led you on.
Ignoring clubs like my favorite song,
Karaoke at dawn,
We both know what eye contact means,
You're singing my song but quietly.

~64~

You didn't try to hurt me,
It's alright.
My minds going places it shouldn't be,
On this night.
The things I'd tell you if you were around,
The things I'd let you do to me if I was feeling down.

You didn't try to hurt me,
It's alright.
But when I'm down I like a bully,
This is my life.
The night's gone weak like I've been all week,
My mind's going places it shouldn't be,
You're fucking with a stranger instead of me,
I'm thinking you didn't deserve me.
You're with the boy on the corner on the street.
I want a boy on the corner of the street.

You didn't try to hurt me,
It's alright.
But when I'm down I like a bully.
This is my life.
Even though love never lasts he can still have a blast,
With the boy on the corner of the street.
He'll never be heard again, time won't be a waste,
With the boy on the corner of the street.

Lines and Words

[Enter YOU from the far east corner]
[Enter ME the solace in the seam]

All of the lines and words you've said to me,
Were edited to fit your needs.
There's countless rewrites, but the structures the same.
You exchange "love" for "hate" like you're ashamed to say…

All the lines and words you've fed to me,
I can rebuke the feelings tied to each.
All the halfhearted drafts were all too eager and brave,
Until the one I wrote where your character could break…

The tension and pace can make it known;
You think it's cool to put this love up for show.
Sitting still and still my shoulders cold,
All these lines and words are sitting jokes.

[YOU turn from the back wall]
[ME turning to a new scene]

All the lines and words you've said to me,
Aren't the only things between your teeth.
The script as old as the yellow stains,
I'm ticking the clock all over your face.

Rehearsals are over, there's no room to cry,
No "I can't do this" or "I've forgotten my lines."
Running around as the curtain comes close,
I've played this part well, though I suppose…

All the lines and words you've said to me,
Aren't the only things between your teeth.
All the lines and words you've fed to me,
Are lost in your reality.

[Exit YOU quit running if you can]
[See ME a solace who's smitten TILL BLACK]

JO

Superstar?

I've grown up with you haunting my life,
But absent from it at the same time,
I've lived your words like my mother's,
But yours only got me so far.

When a storm came you got me through it,
Carried me out by your candle wick,
You dried my tears with your ghostly hand
And lifted my spirit.

I fought by your side like you did mine,
No matter the claims they fantasized,
I claimed an armor that no one fought,
And lost all my energy.

I grew pimples, and wrinkles, and warts,
Because I fought this one sided war.
Left ugly inside from all the spite,
And wicked like the witch.

The way you say things you believe in,
Whether it's god, fantasy, or gin,
The way you think makes me wonder,
If you really are a superstar?

The way my world spun changed in seconds,
Prepare for battle; Armageddon.
Could the hate you brought startle a war?
The star is shooting down.

~71~

<u>Agenda</u>

Tender plans and swollen hands,
Stop tending to your mask,
I see that you're planned to a stance,
It's time to hear this digital romance;

Superstar on stage takes their command,
Paid for the talent the forgotten lack,
But sit back and watch the program,
The star will dance and sing the scam.

Producers sham of a concrete brand,
Leaving empty some of the cracks,
Where the artist's wrists have a shackle tan.
The big man has a plan.

The agenda we have –to support the best,
Is taken to dinner then taken to bed,
Their love pulses back to deep in our chests,
Leaving producers with much less stress.

The agenda we have –to worship a few,
Fallen stars who crater a bruise,
We are blind to the whole spectrum of hues,
Valuing the city of stars that fume.

They agenda they have is because of us,
Searching and scanning for our lust.

<u>Stereotype</u>

We are all stereotypes,
You judge me by what you see,
You think I'm mad,
Happy, or sad.

He's coming in the world with,
A purse and a red carpet,
He's begging for the world to change.
Rainbow pouted and plump lips,
Talk in a higher octave,
He thinks it will end with their grave.

She's got the sweetest of voices,
And prompting nonviolence,
Smoking a joint –from her bandana it came.
Her words just as potent,
She claims her only truth is;
She thinks she'll start a road to pave.

He's shaping out the pretty boy,
Goodbye to blatant teenage noise,
Convince them you can be someone with brains.
A muscled sculpture with tan loins,
A kinky metrosexual Freud,
A gallery that all will campaign.

She's running with the violence,
That resides in every silence,
Speaking what comes through her brain.
Her words are commonsense,
And all things feminist,
But people label her as fake.

We are all stereotypes,
You judge me by what you see,
You think I'm mad,
Sadly,
I am what you command.

<u>Hold Your Breath</u>

Common oath like a lover's choke;
You want to achieve internet goals,
While doing so you can barely breathe.

Who hardly knows what they're deserving of?
Million against one in comments section,
People you barely know aren't on your team.

Hold your breath,
See what's next;
Common themes.

Loners are stoked when the press gets hold,
"Leaked" dripping just like a yolk,
They watch as the world can barely breathe.

While murder goes by the hand that holds,
We all hold hope,
People you barely know are on your team.

Hold your breath,
What makes you connect?
Common means.

People of hate take a picture of hate,
No matter the picture, the person, the place;
People are peeking into your dreams.

Now that you've spoiled them you're best friends,
Twenty-four hour show again and again,
Those you adore are on your team.

Hold your breath,
Who's your safest bet?
Common means.

Thespian love with the beauty of noise,
Parted by talent but together by joy,
In the backseat of her dream you believe.

Rummaging heads but alone you'll ploy,
Playing with men and treating them like boys.
It feels like no one is on your team.

Hold your breath,
And take all I have left;
Comments: mean.

<u>Out to Disrespect</u>

No femmes, no fags,
No Asians, no Blacks,
There's nothing quite worse than being told that.

All the people come together,
Let's push them to the left,
Don't listen to their whining,
They're out to disrespect,

All the people I admit,
I haven't been to smart,
I misspeak a lot,
But never want to cause harm.

No femmes, no fags,
No Asians, No Blacks,
Branded in my head like a panic attack.

All the people we'll learn,
And learning takes time,
Try not to beat them down,
Some will learn to mime,

All the people in the world,
Won't agree with me,
While it's good to have honesty,
It's better to find amity.

No femmes, no fags,
No Asians, No Blacks,
On profiles like an applause –a clap.

No femmes, no fags,
No Asians, No Blacks,
There is nothing quite worse than being told that.

Ritual Love Song

Speak up,
Sing a ritual love song.
For the ones,
Who can't find love.

Scream loud,
Sing a ritual love song,
For the ones,
Who've had enough.

Some people don't need a mirror,
They need to be seeing clearer,
Speculate through a lens,
Analyze the spectacle,
Break the glass and condemn,
Yourself as a caroler.

Go about the streets with ardor,
As a puppeteer bring souls to harbor,
Serenade till their hearts content,
Here's the rapture,
There's still room to lament,
Tonight's for our lovers!

JENSEN

Graveyard Engagement

Are you sad?
I'm beginning this epitaph.
It's nice to hear from the other's paths.
It's getting boring though –so here's my stance;

Dear fashion fad,
Or capitalist plan,
Pillar senior girls over high school clans,
While setting another sheep herd trap.

Dear telephone scam,
Or prank callers with a brand,
I won't hear excuses you try to revamp,
To convince me into your program.

Dear modern romance,
Put some tape on this crack,
And your wig before I give it a snatch,
Wave white flags on empty parapets,

Dear party guests,
I'll bring a limousine,
Around the drinks I will convene,
This social slug makes slow progress.

~83~

Dear reverend,
I'll forgive my rancid mess,
Forget the past health esteem,
Commence high carbon cleanse.

My dearest friend,
Take me on a road that ends,
Sniff all the cats as they sniff us back,
We'll love like the whiskers that touch us.

Dear family,
Funerals come and go,
Like the people they're held for,
And their tears that flow.

A graveyard engagement,
No traces of life,
So wicked and hidden,
But still drinking acid rain.

Poets in the underground,
Wearing colors chemists haven't found.
Copper pieces tightly neat and in their sea of love,
Stretching carpets turned to targets for mass media.

Poets in the underground,
Burning bridges with your higher towns.
Supreme specters once were jesters here for open ears,
Now are cracking down their amorous piers.

Knowledge in the underground,
Blood red signatures of hungry hounds,
These albino thieves and hound dogs do sing,
A timeless song that never changes a beat.

Bombings in the underground,
The city walls are coming down.
Take apart the puzzle pieces of this narrative,
Freedom is chaos like this life they live.

Stealing in the underground,
Footsteps of robbers are all around.
Youngest kin can't be appreciative,
With nothing left they can't get away with it.

Riots in the underground,
It's an occupied battleground.
No one around will take their time to care,
So listen up I can get you to compare.

Poets in the underground,
Broken pedestals are all knocked down,
They'll get their fire in a world unknown,
Thieves take it as theirs and label it as gold.

Stand with them and together we untie,
Discrimination at the root if its spine.
A spark will fire their shadows in places,
Albino hogs leave with their paler faces.

<u>Spidered Spit</u>

My mouth speaks of tiny red shoes at the end of black legs,
Belonging to a family of spiders in my head,
Doctors diagnose me with subtle over-exaggeration,
Call me a shame,
Excuse my brain and put me to rest.

The kids in my class learn to hide behind books in fear,
Even the boxes of smudged crayons are filled with tears,
If I do they feel of service to start a mitigation,
But here's the game,
The surprise scare is the ultimate test.

Comfort isn't something my friends can bare to keep here,
At recess the rainbow slide is haunting so I peer,
Nick and Cameron help me keep my playground nightmare close,
I live and know,
My friends keep quiet and try to cope.

All my little friends are content with me staying in my skin,
Keeping my mouth shut brings me happiness.
But if I stay tight my friends will come out my nose,
And as I blow,
I will live with murdering my friends hope.

An arbitrary hazard keeps them in a plastic sheer,
Their Halloween is futile and comes only once a year,
Order in the bubble lets diffuse this congregation,
It is lame,
I'm entitled to my best.

Decades of victim shame get subtly beat down with leer,
This rainbow slide still haunts my mind as subtly queer,
Come out on wood chips with a new reputation,
I will claim,
Spider webs engraved on our crest!

<u>Running in the Dark</u>

Its midnight,
Quarantined–
Pebbles lodged between the toes of my feet.
Shivers from the rainy grass creep to my teeth.
The earths alone with me until my mind is at peace.

I'm rebel,
Furious.
Weakened by lonesome trails of tristesse,
No one can come rescue me –but undoubtedly,
Maudlin hope will faint with years of honesty.

I'm running,
In the dark,
No shoes, no sought, no spark,
No poets to ignite my warranty,
My own didactic spark of honesty.

Come kindred,
Gluttony
Kissed everyone I know to side with me,
Kissed everyone to stay away from the scene,
Fantasy comply, let the poets believe.

Run poet,

Run to me,

I'll let your frisking spit come up boiling,

And light a fire to animus rioting,

I'm running,

In the dark,

With the promise that others will embark,

Soon they'll wish they dowsed our spark.

<u>Sounds from the Streaming</u>

Take her side open,
As the wind breaks free.
Watch as the water clears,
And all her pebbles are there;
Streaming.

Sticking to the sand that binds them,
But drifting from the ripples and wind from your feet.
Are you listening?

The bubbles are popping from;
Her pebbles are screaming sons.
Radiating and pulling you in,
Plucking the plants in her guard;
Feelings.

Slowly the waters turn cloudy,
Missed your chance!
Weren't you listening?

One step wrong,
Pebbles back in place.
Though twisted and twirled,
For reasons unknown they seem the same;
Dreaming.

Glowing like loose change to a hungry thief,

Pebbles aren't pennies; not meant for your spending.

D'you hear the coins plopping?

Men toss their stars,

And she wishes on them.

Walking in the stream,

Pebbles kick them down like seismic suns;

Healing.

Cosmic clouds again,

Carry crossings that twist and strain.

With enough force to make a pearl,

You forge –and forge –and love a world;

Ending.

SASHA

<u>Milieu</u>

Words are lost in the silence we're so comfortable in,
They soak in between filler scenes,
And reek from the carpet.

This smoke will stick to my hands and smell like cigarettes,
While I'm reeling from their benefits;
I'm high for only a minute.

The ticking stops for the clock has lost its madness,
So faded in the background noise,
I've forgotten how it sounded.

A graveyard engagement with no traces of ruin,
Sometimes wicked sometimes hidden,
These are the spaces we live in.

<u>In the Desert</u>

An alarming shriek,
Chimes over something,
And banters over,
The stories we share.

A harrowing form,
From under blazing,
Comes haunting quickly,
And feeding our fear.

I separate first,
With only another,
Watching our backs till morning,
When do we get to mourning?

The nighttime chill,
Breathes down our boney backs.
They skinny up,
Like the devil is near.

As the sun comes up,
And I look into the mere,
I hear the beast tame,
And to myself I say;

It's colder in the wind of the rhyme,
Even more so by your lonesome side.
When the world gets heavy in the middle of the night,
You can see paradise.

My exhausted lips,
Dried into sandstorms.
My body cowers,
Over oceans of land.

My friends are gone,
But the cacti are listening,
They give me a prick,
When I've come distressing.

The beast lays to my side,
While my temple is still,
I arrange a blessing,
By the beast in my ear.

It's getting too hard for me to breathe,
All I see are shapes in the sand stream,
The sun is heavy as I'm trying to survive,
But I keep saying;

It's warmer with my eyes closed tight,
Again the sun hides with its playful light,
But with the star shining bright I realize,
It's paradise.

<u>Sunset Drive in the Winter</u>

Hungry kids under pavilions.
Fragile men and tired women.
Snow angels keep the heavens watching,
Safe shiver –safe slip for careless walking.
Ether.

Lover's warmth: a scammer's million.
A life of bets close happiness curtains.
I'll give you some change for your feelings,
My two cents give change to your savings.
Ether.

Flower beds in this metropolis,
Hide their colors from kids –cancerous.
Bundled and refraining from freezing,
Leaves kids jealous –the weaker are thriving.
Ether.

Every thud is hope that your front door,
Comes a caroling cruise to rest ashore.
For only a second then right back to sailing,
Alone in this house –burnt wallpaper's dancing.
Ether.

As the sun starts to hide it gets cold outside,
The wind starts to chime and things haunt my life.
Shadows sprout as long as they stay haunting,
Snow twinkles disappear until next joyous morning.
Ether.

Elegy for the living scion.
This ether is a greatest murre,
Ether,
Ether,
We hurt.

<u>Flamingo Sky</u>

Do you see it?

The sun hides and it's cold outside,
The wind chimes and things haunt the night,
The crisp brown leave crunch again,
Across the blush an owl sends.

Socks fly high like flags in rhythm,
Scream loud and shriek for nightly fortune,
The kids crawl out to trespass in
The world day riders keep foreign.

Headboards knock and windows swing
To the beat of younglings loving.
Each head rush a journey through time,
Do you see the power of the hour in mind?

Coyote house brings vagabonds;
Their time comes when night has dawned;
With desperate hearts and eager war
They hope their legacy won't be lore.

Satin back black cats will ration
Till what they have turns to fashion;
Style comes –it takes a while;
Hogs will steal it to beguile.

Horse 92 is on the move,
Betting his life on its rouge shoes,
Unknown to mysteriousness,
Rouge shoes fly into his distress.

Twisted virgin likes to pursue
The thoughts of people who assume.
They're keeping up grand barriers,
And marking down who would fuck their.

A ghost by the will of his own
And turned into a flamingo;
He's prone to walk through halls alone;
Searching for the son he calls home.

Come outside to stay alive,
This condition will let us thrive,
The power of this hour in mind,
Do you see it?

<u>Needletown</u>

There's needles popping up like weeds,
My friends walk with tired bare feet,
By means to achieve their harvest.

There's a thread tying me to the seeds,
I can't ignore this tragedy,
But I can despite the pressure.

The list of names grows longer roots,
In newspaper column tributes,
The names I know increase each day.

There's a house down Ray street alley,
Coyote house lures kids with needs,
And leaves them begging for seconds.

Blame them for picking this toxin,
Yourself too because this happened,
But blame is the farthest cure.

Thread the needle through those in town,
Sew the blanket and place the crown,
Of industry pigs who started this.

<u>Spotlight</u>

A crowded shrub takes my dignity away,
I'm not into bugs,
Or any leaves if I must say.

But the tick of my mind finds this landscape,
In a spotlight,
In a foliage frame.

Looking through the frame of this fantastic place,
With all the creatures,
And the woman they claim.

The ocean of robes that cover her face,
Are as deep as it is,
And as nimble as waves.

My feet crunch the leaves –some brittle as fame,
Just as it's bestowed,
On this goddesses mane.

My fingers fringe through the moist space,
Touch the goddess,
And you will go insane.

My heart finds its place in the crevice of craze,
In this spotlight,
And with great amaze:

The player of nature will remain bleak,
For the eyes of man,
See themselves at their peak.

The tallest of mountains are always complete,
They even out,
There's no reason to retreat.

A chaotic balance keeps us at our feet,
We take what we need,
While they replenish their heath.

The dead can act as the living leech,
Alive in our heads,
But unable to beat.

An aperture may rest in the back of our dreams,
It is up to us,
If we stay idle and weep.

The care of her hands bring me to stay,
At the table of lilies,
She showed me the way.

Speaking in a maze of vatic slang,
She gives me hope,
In my unwanted pain.

When most people refute the altruist way,
I wander off,
In the company of this place.

Acknowledgements

Although *The Beloved* celebrates peoples, I would like to thank a few in particular. Firstly, my friends from school: Bridget, Dow, Paulina, and Thankama for teaching me what love means. Together we formed a group of benevolent misfits and tried to help each other through college. I wouldn't be as comfortable with my emotions if it wasn't for your four. You have allowed me to be vulnerable in ways that I was uncomfortable with at first, but have grown to appreciate.

Next, thank you to Mary Kate Kelly, who's currently chasing her dream. Thank you for showing me you can do this, that it isn't just something motivational speakers say. Of all the people who said it on television you are the only one who convinced me it was possible. Your actions speak louder than anyone's words. Thank you for motivating me to do the same.

I would like to thank my family. My sister, Holly. Your loyalty and support that I am so grateful for. After all we've been through I know that at the end of the day you'll be there. To my parents, who have made me the person I am today. I thank you for being there to learn from and helping me chase my dreams. Lastly, thank you Mark at No Frills Buffalo Publishing for opening your doors to artists and giving them the power they deserve.

About the Author

Andrew Hart Benson has a degree in Communication, but this is the only thing he could think of to do with it. After spending most of his life in the classroom he is excited to share his debut novel with whoever will read it. Apart from his debut novel, he is also passionate about his videography. If you're trying to contact Andrew, you can message him or track him down at any local coffee shop.

Email: Andrewhartbenson@gmail.com
Instagram: Andrewhartbenson
Twitter: Andrewhbenson
YouTube: Andrew Hart Benson